YOU CHOOSE
BOOKS

MARS EXPLORATION
R O V E R S

An Interactive Space Exploration Adventure

by Steve Kortenkamp

Consultant:
Harold Pratt
President of Educational Consultants
Littleton, Colorado

CAPSTONE PRESS
a capstone imprint

You Choose Books are published by Capstone Press,
1710 Roe Crest Drive, North Mankato, Minnesota 56003
www.mycapstone.com

Library of Congress Cataloging-in-Publication Data
Names: Kortenkamp, Steve, author.
Title: Mars exploration rovers : an interactive space exploration adventure /
    by Steve Kortenkamp.
Description: North Mankato, Minnesota : You Choose Books, an imprint of
    Capstone Press, [2017] | Series: You choose books. You choose: Space |
    Audience: Ages 8–12. | Audience: Grades 4 to 6. | Includes
    bibliographical references and index.
Identifiers: LCCN 2016009143| ISBN 9781491481066 (library binding) | ISBN
    9781491481394 (pbk.) | ISBN 9781491481431 (ebook (pdf))
Subjects: LCSH: Mars (Planet)—Exploration—Juvenile literature. | Roving
    vehicles (Astronautics)—Juvenile literature. | Space robotics—Juvenile
    literature.
Classification: LCC QB641 .K674 2017 | DDC 523.43—dc23
LC record available at http://lccn.loc.gov/2016009143

Editorial Credits
Adrian Vigliano, editor; Kayla Rossow, designer;
Wanda Winch, media researcher; Laura Manthe, production specialist

Photo Credits
European Space Agency (ESA): Christophe Carreau, 36; Denman Productions, 76; Getty
Images: Liaison Agency/Newsmakers/NASA, 70; NASA, 56, 58, ESA/Hubble Heritage
Team (STScI/AURA), nebula design element, Jet Propulsion Laboratory (JPL), 22, 32,
JPL/Arizona State University, R. Luk, 62, JPL/Ball Aerospace, 42, JPL/Malin Space
Science Systems (MSSS), 50, JPL/NSSDCA, 12, JPL-Caltech, 54, 105, JPL-Caltech/
Cornell/USGS, 82, JPL-Caltech/MSSS, cover, 100, JPL-Caltech/University of Arizona,
41, JPL-Caltech/University of Arizona/Texas A&M University, 88, Kennedy Space
Center, 10, 46, USGS, 6; Science Source: NASA, 18; Shutterstock: HelenField, lunar
surface design, HorenkO, paper design

Printed in Canada.
009634F16

Table of Contents

ABOUT YOUR ADVENTURE

YOU are living through a time of exciting space exploration progress. Engineers and scientists are working with ever advancing orbiters and rovers to explore Earth's neighbor planet, Mars.

In this book you'll explore how the choices people made meant the difference between success and failure. The events you'll experience happened to real people.

Chapter One sets the scene. Then you choose which path to read. Follow the directions at the bottom of each page. The choices you make will change your outcome. After you finish your path, go back and read the others for new perspectives and more adventures.

YOU CHOOSE the path
you take through history.

Humans have long been curious about Mars, one of Earth's closest neighbors.

CHAPTER 1

MYSTERIES OF THE RED PLANET

On the evening of October 30, 1938, Orson Welles performed *War of the Worlds* on the radio. The broadcast was intended to sound like a news program. The first startling words many listeners heard were:

"Ladies and gentlemen, this is the most terrifying thing I have ever witnessed ... Wait a minute! Someone's crawling out of the hollow top. Someone or ... something. I can see peering out of that black hole two luminous disks ... are they eyes? It might be a face. It might be ... [shouts of awe from the crowd]"

Turn the page.

War of the Worlds used sound effects and the voices of actors to pretend Martians were invading Earth. Some listeners panicked, thinking that Earth really was under attack. Many of them even called the police.

Nobody could fault people for believing in Martians in 1938. American astronomer Percival Lowell described seeing canals crisscrossing the planet. Lowell thought Martians were using these canals to carry water to farms and cities across a drought-stricken planet.

During the next 30 years astronomers work to get a better view of Mars. Bigger and better telescopes help a little, but millions of miles separate Earth from Mars. To get a really good look, we need to go to Mars ourselves.

From 1960 to 1971 engineers build and launch 17 different robotic spacecraft toward Mars. Nearly all of them either fail or survive only a short time.

In 1971 engineers finally succeed in placing a spacecraft into orbit around Mars. Pictures sent back to Earth by the Mariner 9 spacecraft don't show any canals. Instead, Mariner 9's cameras reveal dry riverbeds, ancient flood plains, and gigantic canyons. It looks like Mars was once a very wet planet. But there is no sign of water anymore. To discover where the water has gone and search for Martian life would require sending many more spacecraft to Mars.

Turn the page.

In 1975 the National Aeronautics and Space Administration (NASA) prepares to launch a new mission to Mars. NASA designs the Viking missions to include four spacecraft—two orbiters to photograph Mars from space and two landers to study the planet on the ground. NASA will join each orbiter with a lander and launch them to Mars as the twin Viking 1 and Viking 2 missions.

Technicians inspect the Viking 2 lander at the Kennedy Space Center.

On August 20, 1975, Viking 1 launches from NASA's Kennedy Space Center in Cape Canaveral, Florida. Viking 2 leaves Earth three weeks later on September 9. When the Viking twins arrive at Mars, the orbiters and landers will split and begin their separate missions.

You can join the teams working on either part of these exciting missions. The orbiters will examine Mars from space and search for future landing sites for robots and humans. The landers will study the planet's rocks, soil, and air and search for any signs of life.

But be warned, exploring Mars is very risky. Choose the wrong path and your spacecraft could be lost in space or doomed to a fiery crash on the red planet.

To join teams working on Mars orbiters, turn to page 13.
To join teams working on Mars landers, turn to page 59.

Mariner 9 mapped 85 percent of the surface of Mars while in orbit.

CHAPTER 2

ORBITAL INVASION

The 1970s are an incredible time for NASA's space program. NASA teams are exploring the moon and building robots to explore other planets. You dream of working on space missions. That's why you became an engineer—to build the spacecraft exploring new frontiers.

After college, you get a job at NASA. You work on dozens of different projects and get promoted through the ranks. Your ideas greatly improved the Mariner 9 mission that orbited Mars in 1971. Your work on this orbiter comes to the attention of Tom Macklin. He's project manager of the Viking missions at NASA's Langley Research Center in Hampton, Virginia.

Turn the page.

13

Macklin visits your office on September 10, 1975, one day after the launch of Viking 2. "We have 11 months until those Viking spacecraft get to Mars," he tells you. "The engineers at JPL designed the Viking orbiters to last 120 days in orbit around Mars." JPL is NASA's Jet Propulsion Laboratory, in Pasadena, California. That's where Viking was built.

Macklin continues, "That's too short! The scientists want to map the entire planet, and 120 days isn't enough time."

You agree. You remember Mars had a massive global dust storm when Mariner 9 arrived four years earlier. But careful planning by your team allowed the orbiter to wait until the dust began to settle. Then your team began discovering the huge canyons and volcanoes on the surface.

Macklin pulls a long roll of paper from under his arm. He slides a rubber band off the roll and spreads out the paper across your desk. On the paper you see the engineering drawings for the Viking orbiters. Suddenly you realize why Macklin is in your office!

"I want you to join the Viking orbiter team." Macklin says. "Will you help us coax a few more months out of these orbiters?" You shake Macklin's hand and say, "Count me in!"

After nearly a year of work, it's now the summer of 1976. Viking 1 and Viking 2 both arrive at Mars within weeks of each other and begin orbiting the planet. As planned, the twin Viking landers separate from the orbiters. The lander team drops the two Viking landers to the planet's surface. Your orbiter team begins photographing the surface of Mars from space.

Turn the page.

Your planning lets the orbiters conserve the fuel used to keep their solar panels aligned with the sun. The Viking 2 orbiter runs out of fuel and drifts off alignment in the summer of 1978. But your Viking 1 orbiter doesn't run out of fuel until August 7, 1980, after four years orbiting Mars!

Your work allowed scientists to photograph 97 percent of Mars's surface. One of the photos shows a mysterious structure on the surface of Mars. It looks like a face. Who or what created it?

Over the next 10 years you work on several NASA missions, exploring other planets. In 1990 you're promoted to orbital mission manager. NASA lets you choose your first mission. Three Mars orbital missions are planned for the next decade. Which will you choose?

To work on the Mars Observer mission, go to page 17.
To work on the Mars Global Surveyor mission, turn to page 24.
To work on the Mars Climate Orbiter mission, turn to page 32.

Mars Observer will be launched in 1992. Your biggest challenge as mission manager is working with the huge team of engineers that will build, test, and operate the spacecraft.

Scientists working on the project want Observer to study the geology and climate of Mars. To do this, your team includes cameras with many light filters that can detect different types of minerals and rocks on the surface.

You add other instruments to measure the heights of volcanoes and the depths of craters. They will also help scientists measure differences in the amount of water and dust in the atmosphere and record weather patterns.

Observer requires a lot of electricity. From working with Mariner and Viking, you know that solar panels work well for generating this power. You include six solar panels on Observer.

Turn the page.

The scientists also want to keep gathering data when Observer is on the dark side of Mars. Of course, you know that solar panels won't work in the shadow of Mars. They need to be in the sun. Your solution is to include two batteries for storing electricity that can be used at night.

Overall, your team has built Mars Observer to be the most complex orbiter ever sent to explore another planet. It is also one of the most expensive—the cost is more than $800 million.

Mars Observer was launched 17 years after the Viking 1 and Viking 2 missions.

On September 25, 1992, your team gathers to watch the launch at an outdoor viewing area. A countdown clock ticks down, then powerful engines on the Titan III rocket light up. You feel a shock wave rattle through your body.

After launch, a hand grabs your shoulder. The hand belongs to Dan Silver, the head of NASA and your boss. He tells you how impressed he is with how you managed the Observer team.

"NASA has two more Mars orbiter missions that we're just starting to design," Silver tells you. "They'll use technology that has never been tried before. You can stay with the Mars Observer team to see your first mission through all the way to Mars. Or you can help with one of these new missions."

To stay with your Mars Observer team, turn to page 20.
To move on to Mars Climate Orbiter, turn to page 32.
To move on to Mars Odyssey, turn to page 38.

It is August 21, 1993. After 11 months, Mars Observer is finally nearing Mars. Everyone is anxious about this phase of the mission. The team has spent years preparing for this moment.

The approach to Mars is fast—nearly 40,000 miles (64,374 kilometers) per hour. The spacecraft needs to fire its rockets in order to slow down enough to go into orbit around Mars. If the rockets don't fire, it will go past Mars into empty space, never to return. Computer programmers on your team have sent instructions to the spacecraft to pressurize the fuel tanks, so the rockets will be ready to fire.

As mission manager, you speak to the press. A reporter has pulled you aside for an interview about your mission. You explain how your team uses radio signals to control Mars Observer.

"How long does it take for the signals to reach Mars Observer?" she asks.

"Even at the speed of light, it still takes about 5 to 10 minutes for the signals to travel across the solar system to where Mars is right now," you say.

"So after Observer follows the commands, it sends a signal back to NASA on Earth? And that takes another 10 minutes to get back?" she asks.

"Yes," you say. "And these times are approximate. We should hear back from Mars Observer between 10 to 15 minutes after we send the command to pressurize the fuel tanks."

You rejoin your team in the control room. Just 10 minutes have passed. After 15 minutes no radio signal has come back. You begin sweating. After 20 minutes there is still no signal.

After one hour, the team tries sending a new signal every 20 minutes. No signals ever return. NASA never hears from Mars Observer again. The $800 million mission is nearly a total loss.

Turn the page.

Your team of engineers must now help investigate what went wrong. You go through all the evidence. As the mission manager, it's your job to tell Dan Silver what you think happened.

"Dan, the only thing we can come up with is that a fuel line must have ruptured during the fuel tank pressurization. Nothing else makes sense," you tell Silver.

"How would that have caused the loss of the mission?" Silver asks.

Mars Climate Orbiter was designed to spend two years studying the planet's atmosphere and mapping the surface.

You explain, "The leaking propellant would have acted like a small thruster on the side of the spacecraft. It would have sent Mars Observer spinning out of control. Without the ability to keep its antenna pointed at Earth, it couldn't send a signal back to report the problem. And we couldn't contact it either."

Silver nods. Both of you remember other failed Mars missions. "At least with Mars Observer we have a good idea of what happened. That'll help you do better next time," Silver says.

"Next time!?" you ask. You worry Silver might fire you, but he's giving you another chance!

Silver smiles. "I've got two more Mars orbiter missions that need a new mission manager. It's not too late to join Mars Climate Orbiter, or you can take the new Mars Odyssey mission."

To take Mars Climate Orbiter, turn to page 32.
To take Mars Odyssey, turn to page 38.

The twin Viking missions were unusual successes. Of the 21 missions to Mars before 1975, 14 failed for one reason or another. That means you have a big task ahead of you. Mars Global Surveyor (MGS) needs to succeed. One of its mission objectives is to scout landing sites for future landers, rovers, and, eventually, humans.

Scientists designing MGS are building six instruments for the orbiter to carry to Mars. One of the critical instruments is the Mars Orbiter Laser Altimeter (MOLA). David Schmidt is MOLA's lead scientist.

You meet with Schmidt in his office at NASA's Goddard Space Flight Center in Greenbelt, Maryland. "Tell me about MOLA," you say.

"Yes, MOLA … well the critical part is really the L, which stands for Laser," Schmidt explains. "You see, MOLA fires a laser from the orbiter down to the surface of Mars. Then a small detector on MOLA can see the reflection of the laser off the surface. MOLA times how long it takes for the laser to go from the orbiter to the surface and then reflect back up to the detector."

You finish his thought. "So the laser travels at the speed of light. By timing how long it takes to reach the surface and bounce back to the orbiter, you know how far away the surface of Mars is."

"Exactly! We'll shine that laser down to Mars millions of times, even billions! By the end of the mission, we'll have built a complete elevation map of the entire planet!" Schmidt says enthusiastically.

Turn the page.

"But there's one important thing," Schmidt adds. "A big engine is needed to reach Mars and then slow the Surveyor down so that it will go into orbit around Mars. But the mission can't afford to use big rockets like the Viking orbiters did. NASA didn't give us enough money for that. So how do you intend to get the spacecraft into a good orbit around Mars without those rockets?"

"I have two ideas," you tell Schmidt. "The first is a new lightweight rocket engine, but it's never been tested in space."

"That sounds kind of dangerous. What's your other idea?" Schmidt asks.

"It's a risky maneuver called aerobraking," you reply.

To try aerobraking, go to page 27.
To try the new lightweight rocket engine, turn to page 56.

26

Aerobraking involves flying the spacecraft through the upper parts of a planet's atmosphere to slow it down. The MGS will slow down when the atmosphere of Mars hits the solar panels and resists the forward motion of the spacecraft.

When MGS reaches Mars, it will first go into a long, stretched-out elliptical orbit. Each time it passes closest to Mars, it'll dip into the top of the atmosphere. Aerobraking will slow it down. Gradually the elliptical orbit will evolve into a small, almost circular orbit. Then MOLA and the other science instruments will start to collect data.

Using rockets to regulate MGS's orbit is very expensive because the rockets add weight. Aerobraking is free, but it's very risky. If the calculations are wrong, the spacecraft could be damaged or destroyed.

Turn the page.

The engineers and scientists on your team think it's worth the risk. If aerobraking works at Mars, then future spacecraft can use it too. That would save NASA nearly $250 million on this mission, and billions more dollars in the future.

On November 7, 1996, Mars Global Surveyor blasts off from NASA's Kennedy Space Center. It begins its long trip along a curved path toward Mars. The journey will take more than 10 months. That's a long time to wait.

After Global Surveyor is on its way, you have a visitor at your office at NASA headquarters in Washington, D.C. It's your boss, Dan Silver. Silver has headed NASA since President George Bush appointed him in 1992. He's impressed with how you led the Global Surveyor mission. Silver wants you to lead another mission, the Mars Climate Orbiter.

To stay with Global Surveyor until it gets to Mars, go to page 29.
To move on to Mars Climate Orbiter, turn to page 32.

Aerobraking is risky, but you've done it before. You were part of the Magellan mission in 1993 that used this type of aerobraking for the first time. Magellan used it to get into orbit around the planet Venus.

Global Surveyor arrives at Mars on September 12, 1997. Your team starts with a long, stretched-out orbit that takes nearly two days for just one trip around the planet. During each orbit, Global Surveyor passes ever so slightly into the upper part of the Martian atmosphere. The drag of atmospheric pressure on the solar panels slows the spacecraft a tiny bit, causing the orbit to get smaller.

After a month of aerobraking, you get an unexpected phone call from Maria Shellfer. She's one of your mission-planning engineers working at JPL in California.

Turn the page.

"We have a problem," she says calmly. "We had to stop the aerobraking. We just realized that one of the solar panels on Global Surveyor was damaged during launch. Aerobraking is causing the panel to bend backward."

You and Schellfer work with the other JPL engineers to come up with a new plan. You decide that the aerobraking will have to be a bit gentler. Global Surveyor won't be able to dip so low into the atmosphere. It will take longer to reach a small, stable orbit, but the mission can continue.

Finally, in March 1999, you get another call from Shellfer. "We did it! Global Surveyor is now in a two-hour circular orbit around Mars," she says. "We're turning on the science instruments!"

David Schmidt is excited to hear the news. He'll finally be able to fire MOLA's lasers at Mars.

You wonder what your next Mars mission will be. There is a new orbiter being planned. This one is called Mars Reconnaissance Orbiter (MRO). It will include the most powerful telescope ever sent to Mars. The MRO telescope will be able to see details as small as a footprint—not that you expect to find any footprints on Mars.

Just then, there's knock on your office door. You look up to see Jana Barett standing there. Barett is a NASA geologist at JPL. She loves rocks, especially the Martian kind. She is also on a JPL team that is building two robotic rovers to drive around on Mars.

Barett has a favor to ask. "We need your help with Global Surveyor. We want to use your orbiter to communicate with the new rovers that will be driving around on Mars."

To move on to Mars Reconnaissance Orbiter, turn to page 42.
To stay with the Global Surveyor team, turn to page 52.

Dan Silver, the head of NASA, has reorganized the Mars exploration program. He has seen too many expensive failures that force NASA back to the drawing board. Silver wants more missions to Mars, but he also wants to make them better and less expensive.

Calling for, "faster, better, and cheaper," he puts NASA on schedule to launch two spacecraft to Mars every time Earth and Mars line up on the same side of the sun. That happens about every two years. His plan includes sending two missions for the cost of one.

Mars Pathfinder's rover, Sojourner, operated on Mars 12 times longer than expected.

The first two missions were a huge success. Mars Global Surveyor and Mars Pathfinder arrived at Mars in 1997 and worked exactly as planned. Looking ahead to 1999, Silver has assigned one engineering team to the Mars Polar Lander mission. He asks you to lead the 1998 Mars Climate Orbiter team.

Scientists want to use Climate Orbiter to search for water and ice on Mars. They also want to monitor the daily weather patterns for signs of past long-term climate change.

You and the team of scientists have built two instruments. The infrared radiometer will measure changes in heat in Mars' atmosphere. The Mars color imager will use two cameras to take pictures of the planet's surface and atmosphere.

Turn the page.

Your lead engineer on the Climate Orbiter spacecraft is Beth White. She's been talking with Paul Sloane, who is her counterpart on the Polar Lander spacecraft. White and Sloane both come to you with a plan.

"Dan Silver says we have only $325 million total for both of these missions," White begins.

You nod, "Yes, and almost $100 million of that is for the rockets to launch them off Earth. It doesn't leave us much for the spacecraft."

"Paul and I have come up with a way to cut down on the weight of the lander and reduce its cost," says White.

Sloane then speaks up, "Both spacecraft don't need to be able to communicate with Earth. Only the orbiter does."

Sloane sees the puzzled look on your face. He continues, "We can use the orbiter to relay signals from Earth to the lander. It works the other way too. The lander sends signals to the orbiter, then the orbiter sends them back to Earth."

"That's a great idea," you reply. Only the orbiter will need the big circular antenna for communicating with Earth. The lander can use a smaller antenna. That will save on weight, which translates into fuel savings. It'll save tens of millions of dollars.

White and the rest of your engineers get back to work building the orbiter. They add fuel tanks, rocket engines, and thrusters for maneuvering. A small computer will control the instruments and engines and process the commands sent from Earth.

Turn the page.

The team attaches three solar panels to supply electricity to the instruments and computer. When Climate Orbiter arrives at Mars, these panels will produce about 500 watts of electricity.

Finally, at the bottom of the spacecraft, near the Mars color imager, you install rechargeable batteries. When Climate Orbiter is on the night side of Mars, the batteries will supply electricity to the computer and instruments. During the day, the solar panels will recharge the batteries.

An aerobraking spacecraft uses friction from the atmosphere to slow down and to trim its orbit.

You've also designed the solar panels to serve another purpose. After Climate Orbiter arrives at Mars, it will gently skim through the upper part of the atmosphere during each orbit. NASA calls this maneuver aerobraking. Aerobraking is a way to change the size and shape of the spacecraft's orbit around Mars without using expensive fuel.

Climate Orbiter launches on December 11, 1998, safely stored in the nosecone of a Delta II rocket. The long journey to Mars will take more than nine months.

Dan Silver tends to show up in your office the day after you launch a spacecraft. This mission is no different. The faster part of "faster, better, cheaper" is pushing NASA toward the next mission—Mars Odyssey. Silver gives you a choice. Stay with Climate Orbiter or join the Odyssey team as mission manager.

To move on to Mars Odyssey, turn to page 38.
To stay with Climate Orbiter, turn to page 46.

You made a wise choice in joining the Mars Odyssey team. One of your other options, Mars Climate Orbiter, ended in disaster when the spacecraft was lost. An investigation revealed that two teams of engineers had mixed up metric and English units.

Scientists have a lot riding on the Odyssey mission. One goal is to determine where the missing water and ice is hiding on Mars. They are hoping that finding the water will help them determine if life exists or ever existed on Mars.

A molecule of water has two hydrogen atoms and one oxygen atom bound together. That's why water is called H_2O. Odyssey will search for water by looking for the hydrogen in H_2O in the soil.

To search for hydrogen, scientists will use an instrument called a Gamma Ray Spectrometer (GRS). Bill Bingham built the GRS for Odyssey.

"The GRS is a tricky little instrument," Bingham explains. "It detects radiation called gamma rays coming from hydrogen in the soil of Mars. But it will also detect gamma rays coming from the Odyssey spacecraft."

"To avoid radiation from the spacecraft, we need your team to put the GRS about 6 meters away from the rest of the spacecraft," Bingham tells you. "That's about 20 feet, in case your engineers don't know how to convert meters to feet," he adds with a smile.

Bingham loves teasing engineers about the metric mix-up that doomed the Mars Climate Orbiter. You know that humor can be a good way to move past the mistakes of that mission.

Turn the page.

"Don't worry, Bill," you say. "We've come up with a great place for your GRS. We call it the GRS Boom."

Your team of engineers designed the GRS Boom to slowly expand out of the spacecraft after it arrives at Mars. The boom is spring-loaded. Bingham's GRS instrument is attached to the end of the boom.

Your team adds some other instruments, including a heat-sensing camera called THEMIS, to measure the temperature on the surface of Mars. An antenna for communicating with Earth and a group of solar panels are the final additions. To protect the delicate instruments from the extreme heat and cold of space, you wrap the spacecraft in a gold-colored insulating blanket.

Mars Odyssey is now ready to be shipped to NASA's Kennedy Space Center for launch. You can stay on the team once Odyssey gets to Mars. Or you can join a new mission called Mars Reconnaissance Orbiter (MRO). MRO will carry the most powerful telescope ever sent to Mars. The telescope will search for landing sites for new robots being sent to the surface of Mars.

Mars Reconnaissance Orbiter used special equipment to photograph a huge dust devil on the surface of Mars.

To move on to Mars Reconnaissance Orbiter, turn to page 42.
To stay with Mars Odyssey, turn to page 51.

The main scientific instrument on the Mars Reconnaissance Orbiter is the High Resolution Imaging Science Experiment. HiRISE is much different than the tiny camera that was on Mariner 9, your first Mars mission.

Alan McNally is the lead scientist working on HiRISE. The two of you are working together to fit the big telescope into the Reconnaissance Orbiter.

HiRISE is one of six science instruments on the Mars Reconnaissance Orbiter.

McNally explains HiRISE to you. "First, the mirror inside the telescope is about 2 feet (0.6 m) across. Second, instead of a global map of Mars, we're only going to cover a tiny fraction of the surface, just a few percent. I know that doesn't seem like very much, but we'll be able to see amazing detail. With the extra magnification of that big telescope, HiRISE will be able to spot features smaller than a basketball! Even from hundreds of miles up in orbit!"

McNally continues, "We'll see tiny features in the dry river channels, and features on sand dunes and the bottoms of former lakes, and features inside impact craters."

Since McNally is sitting at your desk, you turn your monitor around to face him. With a few clicks, you bring up the spacecraft design.

Turn the page.

In some ways Mars Reconnaissance Orbiter's design resembles a soaring seagull. HiRISE will be installed in the belly of the seagull, with the telescope pointing down at Mars. A large, round radio antenna forms the head of the seagull. You think that is appropriate, because the antenna is how the spacecraft communicates with Earth.

The wings of the seagull are your favorite part. They each have a large solar panel that is angled slightly downward. These gull wing solar panels will be used in aerobraking to put the orbiter in a circular orbit around Mars. That's a trick you first tried with Mars Global Surveyor, and it's worked perfectly every time since then.

You and McNally watch the MRO launch from Kennedy Space Center in Florida. In seven months it arrives at Mars and begins eight months of aerobraking. Then it's ready to begin its mission.

One thing on Mars that you've always been interested in seeing again is the facelike feature. Your old Viking orbiter team first took pictures of it way back in 1976. With the HiRISE camera, scientists will be able to get a very clear look at the face.

But before HiRISE can look at the face, you learn that there is a new danger facing all spacecraft orbiting Mars. It's coming from deep space and heading toward Mars at more than 126,000 miles (202,777 km) per hour!

You're the Mars orbital expert. You could help NASA deal with this new threat. But you also really want to see what that face looks like with HiRISE.

To stay with HiRISE, turn to page 49.
To help NASA deal with the new threat, turn to page 54.

Today is September 23, 1999. You're still leading the Mars Climate Orbiter mission, now nine months after launch.

Slowing Climate Orbiter down so it can slip into orbit around Mars is the most critical moment in the entire mission. You remember the loss of the Mars Observer spacecraft and all of the missions that failed before that. You can't wait for this day to be over.

Mars Climate Orbiter was launched on December 11, 1998, after a one-day delay to fix a software problem.

Your Colorado-based team calculates how many pounds of force the rocket engine should exert in order to place the orbiter perfectly. Their numbers are then sent to another team of your engineers at NASA's Jet Propulsion Laboratory (JPL). That team programs the numbers as computer commands and then sends them through space to Mars Climate Orbiter.

In about 10 minutes, the signal reaches the spacecraft. Climate Orbiter's rocket ignites. Ten minutes later JPL receives a radio signal back from the Orbiter. But something isn't right. The spacecraft is way too low. It's too close to Mars!

During the next 30 minutes, you get increasingly bad reports from your team at JPL. Instead of going into orbit around the planet, the spacecraft entered the atmosphere and then contact was lost.

Turn the page.

It doesn't take long for your two teams to figure out what went wrong. Your engineers in Colorado calculated pounds of force. But your JPL engineers assumed the numbers were in metric Newtons, not pounds. The Colorado numbers simply needed to be multiplied by 4.48 before being sent to the spacecraft. But that didn't happen.

It was simple math that a grade-school student could have done. But without it, the rocket thrust was much too weak. About $125 million worth of spacecraft was lost.

As mission manager, it was your job to prevent this mistake. You take full responsibility and resign from your job at NASA.

THE END

To follow another path, turn to page 11.
To read the conclusion, turn to page 101.

You're visiting Alan McNally's office at the University of Arizona. He's showing you HiRISE images of the surface of Mars.

"We're seeing all kinds of features changing on Mars. Sand dunes are migrating, new craters are forming, gullies are being created by some kind of fluid! It really is amazing," he says.

"Great. But I want to see the face!" you say.

"Ah, yes, the face from Viking. You want to know if there really are intelligent Martians carving giant faces," McNally says with a laugh.

McNally brings up an image on his computer screen. He points and explains, "The sun is shining from left to right, from a rather high angle. In the Viking image, the sun was very low and shining from the top to bottom."

"That doesn't look like a face to me," you say.

Turn the page.

"Nope," McNally says. "It's just a small mountain with some erosion features on the top. There are lots of mesas like this in the deserts here in Arizona. But there could still be life on Mars—just not the advanced race of Martians that Orson Welles wrote about in *War of the Worlds*. We'll keep sending missions to find out if anything ever lived there."

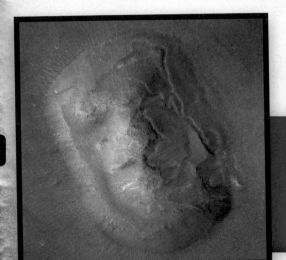

Images from HiRISE helped explain the mysterious face on the surface of Mars.

THE END

To follow another path, turn to page 11.
To read the conclusion, turn to page 101.

After a six-month journey to Mars and three months of aerobraking, Odyssey begins studying Mars. You help use the THEMIS and GRS instruments to build a map of the planet. The Odyssey maps will help NASA pick landing sites for spacecraft to be sent down to the surface.

NASA has also found a new way to use the big radio antenna your team installed on Odyssey. The robots exploring the surface of Mars send their pictures and data up to Odyssey. Then Odyssey relays the information back to Earth. It's become a telecommunications satellite for Mars.

Your Mars Odyssey spacecraft goes on to set the record for the longest surviving Mars mission. It's been there for 15 years and is still going strong. You're proud to have been involved in such a successful part of the space program.

THE END

To follow another path, turn to page 11.
To read the conclusion, turn to page 101.

NASA has sent two rovers named Spirit and Opportunity to Mars. The new rovers don't have large antennas. Instead, most of their images and data will be sent up to your Mars Global Surveyor orbiter. Global Surveyor will then use its big antenna to send the signals to Earth.

Landing is the most critical part of the rover missions. The rover team wants to relay signals to Earth during landing. But Global Surveyor takes nearly two hours to orbit Mars. And the orbiter will be on the other side of Mars at the time the rovers are landing. You'll need to change the orbit by nearly an hour to be in the right place to communicate with the rovers.

You have about 90 days to change the orbit. You tweak Global Surveyor's path by just 3 seconds per orbit. Each day, that adds up to 36 seconds. In 90 days, that will be 54 minutes.

Your math is correct. By January 4, 2004, the first rover lands on Mars just as Global Surveyor is passing overhead. The second rover will arrive January 25. You tweak the orbiter's path a bit more to move it perfectly into place for the next rover landing.

Mars Global Surveyor goes on to great success. The MOLA instrument fires its laser and builds up a global map of the elevation on Mars. It shows the heights of huge volcanoes and the depths of giant craters and canyons.

After nearly 10 years orbiting Mars, NASA loses contact with Global Surveyor in 2006. It is the longest operating Mars mission yet. You're proud that your aerobraking plan was able to make the mission such a huge success.

THE END

To follow another path, turn to page 11.
To read the conclusion, turn to page 101.

On January 3, 2013, your phone rings. When you answer a voice on the other end says, "This is Robert McCabe, and NASA has a problem!" McCabe explains, "I'm an astronomer working at Siding Spring Observatory in Australia. We just discovered a comet heading straight for Mars!"

McCabe names the comet Siding Spring. It will pass very close to Mars. All the dust and gas coming off the comet could damage NASA's spacecraft orbiting the red planet.

Three spacecraft obtained the first up-close observations of a comet flyby of Mars when Siding Spring passed by.

You and your team of engineers make small changes to the spacecraft orbits, just a few seconds per day. These changes add up over the next few months to ensure the orbiters are all on the opposite side of Mars as the comet passes by. Siding Spring slips past Mars on October 19, 2014. Every orbiter survives the comet's passage.

There's even some bonus science from the comet's passing. Scientists use some of the spacecraft to study the comet. One orbiter gets images of a meteor shower caused by comet dust entering the Martian atmosphere.

Siding Spring moves back out into the cold outer reaches of the solar system. McCabe says it won't return for more than a million years, if ever.

THE END

To follow another path, turn to page 11.
To read the conclusion, turn to page 101.

A normal rocket engine uses chemical fuel to create thrust. They've been used for all previous space missions. But these engines and their fuel are heavy and expensive to launch.

The new rocket engine you want to try is called an ion drive. Ion engines use electricity to fire atoms of a gas called xenon out of a small nozzle. Ion engines and their xenon fuel are lightweight. They won't cost much to launch or to use. But they're untested in space. You'll be taking a risk putting them on the Mars mission.

Engineers continue to work on improving thrusters for future space exploration with technology such as ion drives.

Before you can put an ion engine on the spacecraft, you need to test one on the ground. That means you'll have to build one extra engine for testing and another engine for the spacecraft. So it will cost twice as much to use the new engine than you thought it would.

Testing the new engine also means delaying the launch to Mars. If the delay lasts longer than a couple of weeks, the mission will have to wait two years before Earth and Mars are lined up again.

Dan Silver, your NASA boss, realizes that trying this new engine wasn't a good decision. He replaces you with a different mission manager who plans to use the aerobraking technique.

THE END

To follow another path, turn to page 11.
To read the conclusion, turn to page 101.

After deploying on the Martian surface, the two Viking landers took photographs, collected data, and conducted three biology experiments designed to look for possible signs of life.

CHAPTER 3

ROBOTS ON THE GROUND

It is the summer of 1976. Americans are celebrating the country's 200th birthday, the bicentennial. It is an exciting time, especially for a young scientist like you. NASA has just hired you for your first job.

At NASA the celebrations in the summer of 1976 have extra meaning. Twin spacecraft Viking 1 and Viking 2 have just arrived at the planet Mars. Each spacecraft has separated into an orbiter and a lander. In July the Viking 1 lander will attempt to gently drop down to the surface of Mars. No spacecraft has ever done this before.

Turn the page.

You are a part of the Viking 1 lander team. You've traveled with other scientists to a testing site in the California desert. Here, NASA uses an exact copy of the spacecraft to test procedures you will use with the lander on Mars.

You're a bit surprised at how big the three-legged lander is. It's nearly the size of a small car. Most of the lander is coated with gray rubbery paint to protect it from windblown Martian sand.

The radio communication antenna reaches taller than you stand and the robotic arm is longer than both your arms together. The antenna and arm are tested with the same signals and commands that will be sent to Mars in the next few days.

In July, Tom Macklin gathers the Viking team at the Jet Propulsion Laboratory (JPL) in Pasadena, California. JPL is the home of Viking Mission Control. Macklin is NASA's manager leading the entire Viking program.

Macklin's team includes engineers on the Entry, Descent, and Landing (EDL) team. EDL engineers may have the most important job of any planetary landing missions. If the EDL team screws up, the landers will burn up in the Martian atmosphere or crash into the surface. You're glad you don't have to work with that kind of pressure.

On July 20 the EDL team sends commands to Viking 1 to fire its main engine and begin the entry, descent, and landing sequence. As the entire world watches, they guide Viking 1 to a successful landing.

Turn the page.

Viking 1 lands on the gentle slopes of a region named Chryse Planitia. The Greek name means "plains of gold." Everyone at JPL is eagerly waiting to see the first pictures from the surface of Mars. You're watching the control room screens with Tim Nather. He's the scientist who built the cameras on the Viking 1 lander.

Vast amounts of water once flowed through the Kasei Valles and emptied in the Chryse Planitia.

As the first images come back from Viking, the screen begins filling line by line. You and Nather see a pale brown sky and the dish of the communication antenna. As the lines progress, the distant horizon of Mars suddenly appears. Then rocks and soil near the lander come into view. Finally, the image shows instruments on the lander and the American flag painted on a side.

The team at JPL's Mission Control are excited to see the first pictures from the surface of Mars, confirming their hard work with the lander. At the same time you and the other scientists feel deeply disappointed at how lifeless Mars looks.

Of course, you hadn't expected to see little green Martians. But these plains look barren. This scene repeats itself as more images came down from Viking 1, and six weeks later from the Viking 2 lander on the other side of Mars.

Turn the page.

There was no sign of life at all in any of the Viking images. No plants or animals were visible. Scientists use the robotic arm to scoop and test the Martian soil. It doesn't contain even tiny microorganisms such as bacteria. Despite how wet and lively scientists thought Mars might be, the images show a cold desert planet.

Mars is never far from your thoughts as you work on other space missions. You become part of the science teams that parachute a probe into Jupiter's atmosphere and send a lander to the surface of Titan, a giant moon of Saturn. Then NASA announces two new missions to Mars. Mars Polar Lander will search for water near the south pole of Mars. Mars Pathfinder involves launching a small rover to study land formations.

To join the Mars Pathfinder team, go to page 65.
To join the Mars Polar Lander team, turn to page 71.

Today is July 4, 1997. Twenty-one years have passed since the Viking landers became the first missions to land on Mars. After that long absence, NASA is returning to Mars with Pathfinder. Pathfinder holds a small six-wheeled rover named Sojourner that can drive on the planet's surface.

Attached to the front of Sojourner is your science instrument, the Alpha Particle X-ray Spectrometer (APXS). You designed APXS to fire alpha particles at rocks. An alpha particle is just a helium atom without any electrons. When the particles hit the rock, atoms inside the rock give off X-rays. APXS measures these X-rays to determine what kind of rock it is.

Turn the page.

You want to study rocks on Mars, but the Pathfinder mission is more about engineering than science. NASA is using Pathfinder to test a new low-cost technique for landing on Mars. If Pathfinder is successful, future missions can use a similar technique. That will save NASA hundreds of millions of dollars.

Tammy Spalter is NASA's project manager for Pathfinder. She works at JPL. You're at JPL today with the entire Pathfinder team of scientists and engineers. As the landing time approaches, Spalter talks to reporters gathered at JPL about the new landing technique.

"Pathfinder doesn't have large descent engines like the Viking landers," Spalter tells the reporters. "Instead, we borrowed an idea from the cars that most of you drive."

She's referring to car airbags. Pathfinder and the Sojourner rover it's carrying are surrounded by 24 giant airbags. After slowing down in the Martian atmosphere, the airbags will inflate and Pathfinder will drop to the surface. The airbags will cushion its landing.

In the JPL mission control room, the EDL team is waiting for the signal from Pathfinder. The EDL leader motions to Spalter and gives her a thumbs-up sign. Then the announcement from EDL comes, "Touchdown confirmation, Pathfinder has landed!"

After landing, the airbags are deflated and pulled under the lander. Then Pathfinder opens like a three-petal flower. Each petal is a solar panel for generating electricity. The little Sojourner rover then drives off small ramps that unfold from one of the petals.

Turn the page.

Sojourner drives over to a large rock that you and the other scientists nickname Barnacle Bill. Your APXS instrument starts zapping the rock with alpha particles and measuring the X-rays.

The APXS data reveals that Barnacle Bill contains minerals that include quartz and feldspar. Geologists on your APXS team say that this means the rock is probably from a Martian volcano. That could mean there are active volcanoes on Mars today.

In the JPL mission control room, Spalter is quietly talking to another NASA official you recognize but have never seen in person. Dan Silver is the head of NASA. As NASA employs more than 50,000 people, it isn't surprising that you have never met him.

Silver turns to face the Pathfinder team. "The old Viking missions in 1976 cost NASA more than $3 billion to complete," Silver says. "But what you did today with Pathfinder only cost $300 million."

You quickly do the math in your head. With relatively low-cost missions like Pathfinder, NASA can send 10 missions to Mars for the same cost as Viking.

Silver calls this plan "Faster, better, cheaper!" He has NASA on a schedule to launch two spacecraft to Mars every time Earth and Mars line up on the same side of the sun. That happens about every two years. His plan includes sending two missions for the cost of one.

Silver says, "We've got more missions ready to go to Mars. And we need people just like all of you to help with them."

Turn the page.

You have several choices. NASA is sending a lander to the south pole of Mars to search for water under the soil. They are also building two identical twin rovers much larger than Sojourner. The European Space Agency (ESA) also needs help with their Mars Lander, named Beagle 2.

Team members perform a final check of the Mars Polar Lander before beginning a test.

To join the Mars Polar Lander team, go to page 71.
To join the European Beagle 2 lander team, turn to page 75.
To join the twin Mars Exploration Rovers team, turn to page 79.

Ever since the Viking missions, scientists have suspected the water on Mars may be frozen just beneath the dusty surface. NASA is sending the Mars Polar Lander to the south pole region to investigate. Engineers built a robotic arm for the lander to collect soil samples.

Near the end of the robot arm is the Robotic Arm Camera (RAC). It has eight different colored lamps to light up the soil samples. If there is ice under the soil, you'll be able to see it in the pictures taken with RAC.

Your science instruments on Polar Lander are two miniature landers called microprobes. Before Polar Lander touches down, it'll drop the microprobes. They each carry a tunneling device that will test the soil for water.

Turn the page.

You designed the microprobes with tiny antennas to communicate with the larger Polar Lander. Then Polar Lander will send the signals up to an orbiting spacecraft called Mars Climate Orbiter. At least, that was your plan.

But unfortunately, Mars Climate Orbiter was destroyed by atmospheric pressures instead of going into orbit. Your team had to ask NASA to reposition another spacecraft, the Mars Global Surveyor. The Global Surveyor has been orbiting Mars since 1997. Now it will be called in to relay the signals from Polar Lander back to Earth.

Polar Lander finally arrives at Mars on December 3, 1999. You are in the JPL mission control room watching the EDL team monitor the landing. NASA had already starting building Polar Lander before Pathfinder had confirmed that the airbag technique would work. So Polar Lander is using descent engines to touch down.

During the landing, the microprobes deploy properly. But then something goes wrong. The signal from Polar Lander is lost. NASA tries for weeks to contact Polar Lander. They never get a signal from it again. Nor do they hear from your microprobes. The entire mission has been lost.

NASA's investigation finds that the descent engine didn't work properly because of a software malfunction in the EDL computer program. When the landing legs deployed, a signal was accidentally sent to the onboard computer telling it that Polar Lander was already on the ground. So the engines didn't ignite. But Polar Lander was still higher than a 10-story building above the ground. It fell from that height and smashed on the ground.

Turn the page.

You realize that sometimes Dan Silver's plan for "faster and cheaper" doesn't always go together with "better." If NASA had given the EDL team more funding, they could have tested the software more thoroughly. They might have found the problem and fixed it before it was too late.

More missions are being built and launched, though. The Europeans still need your help with the Beagle 2 lander, and the identical twin rovers need scientists to help with instruments on their robotic arms.

You also have a third opportunity. NASA will use spare parts from the Polar Lander mission to build another lander to go to the north pole region of Mars. This new mission is named Phoenix.

To join the European Beagle 2 lander team, go to page 75.
To join the twin Mars Exploration Rover team, turn to page 79.
To join the Phoenix lander team, turn to page 88.

The ESA hires you to work with their scientists on the Beagle 2 Mars lander. It's named after HMS *Beagle*, the ship Charles Darwin used in the 1830s on his voyage to understand life on Earth. ESA wants to use Beagle 2 to search for signs of life on Mars.

Beagle 2 is about 3 feet (0.9 m) wide. It's designed to land on Mars and open like a flower. Four petals are solar panels. A fifth petal, underneath the four solar panels, holds the radio antenna for communicating with Earth. Beagle 2's main body holds the cameras, science instruments, and a Payload Adjustable Workbench (PAW), which is a robotic arm.

PAW has a small drill and a scoop for sampling rocks and soil. The samples will be dropped into scientific instruments to determine if anything in them is alive.

Turn the page.

You've spent nearly two years working on Beagle 2. Your instrument is PLUTO, the Planetary Undersurface Tool. You designed PLUTO so PAW can deploy it over the side of the lander body. Then PLUTO will use springs to move along the surface like an inchworm. PLUTO is attached to Beagle 2 by a power cable.

When PLUTO arrives at an interesting spot, you'll send a radio command for it to burrow into the soil like a mole. In PLUTO's tip is a small hole for collecting soil samples. Then the soil sample will be tested for anything living.

Beagle 2 was expected to operate for about 180 days, or possibly up to one Martian year (687 Earth days).

A European spacecraft, Mars Express, carries Beagle 2 on its mission. Because ESA doesn't have big enough rockets for a Mars mission, they hitch a ride on a Russian rocket. Mars Express launches from Russia on June 2, 2003.

Six and a half months later, Beagle 2 arrives at Mars. It separates from Mars Express and enters the Martian atmosphere on the morning of December 25. But unfortunately, its signal is lost.

ESA finds that Beagle 2 entered Mars' atmosphere at nearly 12,000 miles (19,312 km) per hour. A heat shield protected it from the fiery entry, then a parachute slowed it down. Airbags cushioned its final drop. But when it was time to open the solar panel petals, something went wrong. Only two petals opened. The others were stuck and covered the radio antenna. That prevented Beagle 2 from communicating.

Turn the page.

Years later a spacecraft orbiting Mars used its camera to find Beagle 2 on the surface. It looks like all it needed was a little help opening the last two solar panels. But without them, your PLUTO science instrument couldn't receive its commands to operate.

You now have a choice to make about your future. You've been offered a job teaching astronomy at your former college, where you can inspire the next generation of scientists. Or you can join another Mars mission. The Phoenix Mars Lander mission will land near the north pole of Mars and search for frozen water under the surface. There are also twin rovers named Spirit and Opportunity hunkered down on the surface of Mars waiting for a huge dust storm to pass over them.

To join the Spirit and Opportunity teams, turn to page 85.
To join the Phoenix lander team, turn to page 88.
To become a college professor, turn to page 99.

Ever since the Viking missions, NASA scientists have known that Mars used to be very wet. But all that water seems to have disappeared millions or even billions of years ago.

Scientists have questions about the water. How long did Mars have water on the surface? Where did all the water go? Did anything ever live in the Martian water? Could anything still be alive on Mars?

To help answer these questions, you're joining a very ambitious mission. The Mars Exploration Rovers are twin spacecraft named Spirit and Opportunity. They will drop down to the surface using the same airbag landing method as the Pathfinder rover.

Turn the page.

Just like the Pathfinder rover, Spirit and Opportunity get their electrical power from solar panels on their backs. But they're much larger than Pathfinder.

Spirit and Opportunity each have a tall white mast with pairs of cameras that look similar to eyes. These cameras let the controllers at JPL see Mars in three-dimensional images.

Each rover has a long robotic arm called the Instrument Deployment Device (IDD). Instruments including microscopes and cameras are located at the end of the IDD. That's where your instrument is as well. It's the Rock Abrasion Tool, but you just call it RAT.

RAT is a spinning tool that brushes and grinds away the outer layers of a rock. After using RAT, other scientists will study the rock. That's one way to find out if the rocks were ever submerged in water.

In the summer of 2003 NASA launches Spirit and Opportunity on separate rockets from Kennedy Space Center in Florida. They arrive on Mars seven months later.

Opportunity lands in a region of Mars called Meridiani Planum. From earlier missions, scientists know that Meridiani Planum may once have been the bottom of a shallow sea. The rocks and soil contain a lot of the mineral hematite. Hematite is a form of iron oxide, or rust. On Earth hematite forms in bodies of water such as oceans, seas, lakes, or even hot springs. Opportunity will search for more clues about the possible ancient Martian sea.

Turn the page.

When Opportunity's landing capsule opens, the rover unfolds its solar panels, mast cameras, and IDD. The first images returning to Earth show that Opportunity landed inside a small crater called Eagle.

Opportunity's first images also show something even more amazing. Eagle crater's floor is covered in what looks like blueberries! They actually are tiny spheres of hematite.

The close-up image of "blueberries" taken by Opportunity showed an area of the Martian surface 1.2 inches (3 centimeters) across.

Opportunity climbs out of Eagle and takes images of its surroundings. Hematite covers the ground all around. Millions of years ago, the entire region must have been a sea or ocean.

Spirit lands on Mars's opposite side, thousands of miles from Opportunity. It lands in a large crater called Gusev. This crater sits at the end of a canyon about the size of the Grand Canyon. NASA sent Spirit into Gusev to search for clues about the canyon's history.

Seventeen days after landing, scientists lead Spirit to a rock nicknamed Adirondack. The rock is covered in a very light layer of dust and a thin, hard coating of minerals. You send commands to the RAT to brush the dust off and grind through the outer coating. Then scientists use a microscope on the IDD to study inside the rock.

Turn the page.

Adirondack turns out to be a surprise. It's an igneous rock called basalt. It wasn't submerged in a lake, but instead has come from a volcano. Your team uses the RAT and microscope to study other rocks in Gusev. Most of them are also volcanic rocks. A nearby volcano must have erupted after the lake dried up. The crater's floor is now covered in rocks from that eruption.

As Spirit and Opportunity continue their missions, a dust storm forms on Mars. The storm soon engulfs the entire planet. Dust in the air blocks sunlight from the solar panels on the rovers. Without electricity, the rovers will stop functioning. Nobody knows when the dust will settle and if the rovers will survive.

Do you want to stay with the rovers and see what happens? Or would you rather join a new mission to search for ice near Mars' north pole?

To stay with the Spirit and Opportunity teams, go to page 85.
To join the new Phoenix Lander team, turn to page 88.

The rovers Spirit and Opportunity are engulfed in a massive dust storm. As the storm clears, NASA regains contact with the twin rovers. But there's a problem. The rovers aren't getting enough power from their solar panels.

Suddenly you have an idea. "What if we have the rovers take selfies?" you say to the JPL engineers. "Have them point their mast cameras straight down and then rotate the mast."

"Oh, I get it!" responds an engineer. She continues your thought. "The cameras will be taking pictures of the solar panels on the rover's back. We can put all the pictures together to make a big rover selfie!"

The selfie commands are sent to the rovers. They use their dwindling battery power to take pictures of their solar panels and send them back to Earth.

Turn the page.

The solar panels should be shiny blue. But the selfies show them covered in red dust. Only a small amount of sunlight is getting through the dust to make electricity for the rovers.

The JPL engineers have no way of cleaning the dust off the solar panels. The robotic arms can't reach that far back. Everyone at JPL is worried the rovers won't survive much longer.

Then a remarkable thing happens. Something on Mars cleans the dust from the solar panels. JPL gets signals from each rover indicating they have nearly full solar power. What could have cleaned them?

The JPL engineers send commands to the orbiting Mars Reconnaissance Orbiter. They want to use the orbiter's powerful HiRISE camera to take images of the areas where the rovers are.

When images come back, you learn what cleaned the rovers. Spinning miniature tornados are moving across the surface. People call them dust devils. They must have moved over the rovers and blown the dust off the solar panels.

With clean solar panels and full power, Opportunity can continue its mission. But Spirit isn't so lucky. One of its wheels is trapped in sand. Even with full power, it can't get out of the sand trap.

You have another choice. You hate to leave the Spirit team now, but you'll get more scientific work done with Opportunity. You could also move on to new missions, such as the Phoenix Lander or a giant new rover called Curiosity.

To join the new Phoenix Lander team, turn to page 88.
To stay with the Opportunity Rover team, turn to page 91.
To join the Curiosity Rover team, turn to page 93.
To stay with the Spirit Rover team, turn to page 98.

Scientists working with NASA's Mars Odyssey orbiter discovered vast amounts of hydrogen just below the dusty surface. Most scientists assumed all this hydrogen is in the form of water molecules frozen as ice. But nobody can be certain until a lander mission goes down to the surface and scoops up the soil to see what is underneath.

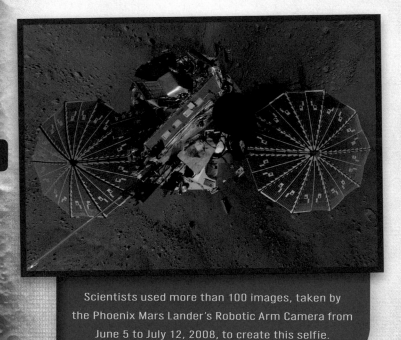

Scientists used more than 100 images, taken by the Phoenix Mars Lander's Robotic Arm Camera from June 5 to July 12, 2008, to create this selfie.

In 1999 Mars Polar Lander was supposed to be that mission. It had a robotic arm with a scoop and a camera. Unfortunately, a tiny glitch in the computer software caused Polar Lander to crash.

Engineers built the Phoenix Lander using many spare parts left over from the Polar Lander and other unlaunched missions. Your contribution to Phoenix is the Robotic Arm Camera (RAC). You designed RAC as a shoebox-sized camera near the end of the robotic arm, just before the scoop. After the arm scoops up soil, RAC will take images of whatever is underneath. Everyone hopes to see ice.

On May 25, 2008, Phoenix lands near the north pole of Mars in a place called Green Valley. Green Valley is where Odyssey detected the highest amount of hydrogen. If there's ice under the soil, this is the place to look.

Turn the page.

Your RAC team of scientists works with the robotic arm team to scoop up soil and take images. Your pictures are clear. It looks like there's a bright layer of ice just below the red, dusty surface of Green Valley.

The robot arm scoops up a sample. Scientists drop the sample into a small oven inside the body of Phoenix. As the sample bakes in the oven, sensors measure the gases it emits. Sure enough, the gases are water vapor.

With Phoenix, NASA has followed evidence of water all the way to the surface of Mars. Seeing the ice just below the surface gives hope to everyone searching for signs of life on the red planet. With further exploration, NASA might find liquid water. You're proud that your designs are part of unlocking the mysteries of Mars.

THE END

To follow another path, turn to page 11.
To read the conclusion, turn to page 101.

JPL's engineers told you Opportunity could only survive about 90 days on Mars. By then the engineers figured the solar panels would be covered with dust. But NASA didn't count on dust devils regularly cleaning off the panels. With help from the dust devils, Opportunity is still going more than 12 years after landing in Eagle crater. But the harsh Martian weather is taking a toll on the rover. Two of its wheels have stopped working. Their motors are frozen in place. As Opportunity drives across Mars, the four good wheels have to drag the two bad ones along.

Your RAT is holding up better than Opportunity's wheels. You use RAT and the microscopes on the end of the robotic arm to study Martian rocks. Many are iron meteorites. Opportunity finds so many meteorites in Meridiani Planum that you joke that Mars is a cosmic junkyard for broken-down asteroids.

Turn the page.

Opportunity is also finding rocks that formed in hot springs on Mars. On Earth, there is a lot of life in hot springs. Finding these rocks could mean that Mars once had life, too.

By now Opportunity has driven 26.4 miles (42.5 km). That's more than the distance of a marathon, which covers 26.2 miles (42.2 km). To some people, that may seem like a long way. But to drive around Mars once would require more than 500 marathons. Opportunity can't explore the whole planet by itself. So NASA is planning bigger and better rovers to keep exploring the red planet and searching for signs of life.

THE END

To follow another path, turn to page 11.
To read the conclusion, turn to page 101.

You join the science operations team for the Mars Curiosity rover at JPL. Nicole Spagnola is the chief of the team. Spagnola is telling you about some of the differences between Curiosity and the older Mars rovers.

"Curiosity is huge compared to Pathfinder," she says. "Just one of Curiosity's wheels is bigger than Pathfinder. The whole rover is the size of my pickup truck, and weighs about as much, too!"

Spagnola knows that you are coming to Curiosity after working with the solar-powered Spirit and Opportunity rovers. The bigger wheels will help keep Curiosity from getting stuck in sand traps like Spirit did. Electrical power won't be a problem for Curiosity either.

Turn the page.

"Curiosity is nuclear powered, instead of solar powered. So we don't need any help from dust devils," she tells you. "We've got at least two years of power for driving and the science instruments, maybe more if we're lucky," she adds.

Just then, there is a knock on the office door. Spagnola introduces you to Adam Spellman, a NASA engineer and leader of Curiosity's Entry, Descent, and Landing (EDL) team. Spagnola asks him to tell you about the technique the EDL team came up with to land Curiosity on Mars.

"Curiosity is so big that an airbag landing wouldn't work for it," he says. "My team designed a rocket sky crane. Using four steerable engines, the sky crane will lower the rover on long cables and gently set it down. Once on the ground, Curiosity will use small explosive blades to cut the cables. Then the sky crane will fly off to a crash landing a safe distance away."

Spellman sees the mixture of excitement and terror on your face. "Don't worry," he says. "Your instruments are in good hands. We've got the best EDL team NASA ever put together."

Curiosity has a large collection of scientific instruments. There are 10 cameras, a robot arm with tools for drilling into rocks, and a microscope for studying minerals. Curiosity's mast has cameras that let the controllers on Earth see images in 3D. The mast also has your instrument, called ChemCam. ChemCam uses a laser to burn holes into rocks. The laser can reach much farther than the robotic arm. You use special cameras on ChemCam and on the robotic arm to study the smoke and powder that comes off the burning rock. That helps you identify what kind of rock it is.

Turn the page.

Curiosity has a laboratory for studying rocks and soil. The robot arm drops samples into the laboratory. One of the experiments heats samples to 1,800 degrees Fahrenheit (1,000 degrees Celsius) and measures the gases that come off. Another uses X-rays to study the samples.

On August 6, 2012, the entire Curiosity team gathers at JPL for the landing. Spellman's EDL team sits in the mission control room waiting for the signals to come back from Mars. Everyone cheers when landing is confirmed.

The science operations team gets right to work. There are images stored in Curiosity's computer that need to be sent back to Earth. Some of the first images contain a new discovery. Curiosity landed in a dried-up stream. The pictures show a thick layer of rock and pebbles, all eroded to round shapes by flowing water.

The water in the stream must have flowed for thousands of years to erode the rocks into the smooth, rounded shapes. You compare pictures of the streambed with streams on Earth. The comparison shows that the Martian stream may have been about hip-deep on a person trying to walk across it.

The next day Curiosity begins driving across the Martian landscape. It is heading for a place called Mount Sharp in the distance. The journey will take more than a year, with Curiosity reaching the lower slopes by 2014. You can't wait to see what the rover will find.

THE END

To follow another path, turn to page 11.
To read the conclusion, turn to page 101.

You want to see if you can help get Spirit out of the sand. As winter on Mars approaches, Spirit needs to climb up the southern slope of a nearby mountain to keep its solar panels in strong sunlight. If it can't make it out of the sand, it won't get enough sunlight to survive the winter.

JPL engineers spend months working to free Spirit. Spirit sends back pictures of its trapped wheels. Engineers use a test rover on Earth to simulate what happened to Spirit on Mars. If they can get the test rover out of the sand, maybe they can learn how to free Spirit.

But nothing works. With its power dwindling, NASA gets the last signal from Spirit on March 22, 2010. Spirit dies in the sand trap six years after landing on Mars.

THE END

To follow another path, turn to page 11.
To read the conclusion, turn to page 101.

You've spent years exploring Mars. Some missions failed. But the successes helped answer old questions and reveal new mysteries about the red planet. As a teacher, you use these mysteries to inspire future explorers of Mars.

You begin each day by telling your class a different story from your experience exploring Mars. Your students explore their own Mars Garden, an area you stocked with rocks, sand, and soil that resembles what you found on Mars. They use some of the instruments you built to test different techniques, like a model Pathfinder and backup PLUTO.

A great teacher inspires students with a sense of wonder. You hope that your classes might inspire your students to work on a human mission to Mars.

THE END

To follow another path, turn to page 11.
To read the conclusion, turn to page 101.

Covering about 660 feet (200 meters) each day, the Curiosity rover was built to roll over obstacles up to 25 inches (65 centimeters) high.

CHAPTER 4

EXPLORATION CONTINUES

Our understanding of Mars has come a long way since *War of the Worlds*. We no longer believe there ever were intelligent Martians who built canals. But Mars certainly was a very wet planet in the past.

All life on Earth uses liquid water in some way. NASA's strategy for searching for life on Mars can be summed up in just three words, "follow the water." The orbiters, landers, and rovers are all being sent to Mars to search for clues about what happened to all that water. The Curiosity rover is still searching inside Gale crater.

Gale crater formed more than 3 billion years ago after an asteroid hit Mars. Over millions of years, rivers flowing from other parts of Mars brought water and eroded sediments to Gale. They formed a huge lake. Layers of mud from the sediments built up each year. When Mars started to dry up, the layers of mud in Gale crater turned into layers of rock. Those rocks hold clues from the past.

After Gale lake dried up, wind and streams eroded the layers of rock. Erosion carved a steep mountain inside Gale crater called Mount Sharp. Curiosity has been slowly climbing the slopes of Mount Sharp since 2015. Scientists will spend years using Curiosity's instruments to study the rock layers. Each layer will tell them something about what Mars was like in the past. In one sample of rock, Curiosity detected nitrogen gas that could be used by bacteria living in the rock.

As scientists work with Curiosity, NASA's engineers are busy building the next Mars rover. The new rover will be launched in 2020. A landing site for the Mars 2020 rover hasn't yet been found, but it will use the same sky crane landing technique the EDL engineers designed for Curiosity.

Mars Odyssey and Mars Reconnaissance Orbiter are still circling Mars. Scientists continue to use their cameras to search for changes in the Martian landscape. One change they've discovered comes from water flowing out of the ground and down the slopes of crater walls. The water is thought to flow in the warmer spring and summer seasons on Mars. Scientists think the liquid water exists underground in aquifers.

A new mission called MAVEN (Mars Atmosphere and Volatile Evolution) recently joined the Mars orbiters. Scientists are using it to study the atmosphere of Mars in order to learn how Mars lost so much water in the past. But studying Mars from space isn't the orbiters' only purpose. They also are relay satellites, getting information from Opportunity and Curiosity and sending it back to Earth. In that way, NASA engineers have built the first network of communication satellites around Mars. These types of satellites will be vital for the next step in Mars exploration, sending humans.

All the orbiters, landers, and rovers studying Mars are paving the way for human astronauts. NASA engineers and scientists are slowly building that capability. The first people may go to Mars in the 2030s. Will you be one of them?

While climbing a high ridge on March 31, 2016, the Opportunity rover photographed a Martian dust devil in the valley below.

TIMELINE

1965: Mariner 4 spacecraft flies by Mars

1969: Mariner 6 and 7 fly by Mars

1971: NASA's first successful Mars orbiter, Mariner 9, returns 7,329 images

1976: Viking 1 and 2 orbiters and landers all succeed, performing the first successful experiments on the surface of Mars

1993: Contact with Mars Observer orbiter is lost just before it arrives at Mars

1997: Mars Global Surveyor reaches orbit, returns more images than all previous missions combined

1997: Mars Pathfinder rover becomes the first rover to operate on Mars

1999: Mars Climate Orbiter crashes

1999: Mars Polar Lander crashes

1999: NASA's pair of Deep Space 2 probes are lost on arrival at Mars for unknown reasons

2002: Mars Odyssey orbiter discovers hydrogen just below the surface of Mars

2003: ESA's Mars Beagle 2 lander is lost on arrival at Mars

2004: NASA's twin Mars Exploration Rovers Spirit and Opportunity both successfully land using the airbag technique

2006: Mars Reconnaissance Orbiter arrives carrying the HiRISE camera, the largest telescope ever sent to study another planet

2008: Phoenix Mars Lander successfully lands near the Martian north pole

2011: NASA stops efforts to free Spirit and officially ends the rover's mission

2012: Mars Science Laboratory mission successfully lands the nuclear-powered Curiosity rover using a rocket-powered sky crane

2014: The MAVEN orbiter arrives at Mars to study the Martian atmosphere

2016: NASA celebrates Opportunity's 12th anniversary of successful operation on Mars

2020: NASA's next generation Mars rover is scheduled to launch

OTHER PATHS TO EXPLORE

In this book, you've seen how events from the past look different from two points of view. Perspectives on history are as varied as the people who lived it. Seeing history from many points of view is an important part of understanding it. Here are ideas for other space exploration points of view to explore:

+ Astronomers living on Earth have been using telescopes to study Mars for more than 400 years. Discuss some of the reasons why using telescopes might be better than using spacecraft, and some of the ways that spacecraft might be better. (Key Ideas and Details)

+ Spacecraft sent to explore Mars can each cost between $100 million and $3 billion. Is it worth spending so much money on spacecraft? What does the exploration of space and other planets teach us? (Integration of Knowledge and Ideas)

+ Each planet that NASA explores is unique. Compare the techniques you read about in this book with techniques for exploring Venus and Jupiter. How do they compare? (Integration of Knowledge and Ideas)

READ MORE

Maxwell, Scott. *Mars Rover Driver.* The Coolest Jobs on the Planet. Chicago: Raintree, 2014.

Miller, Davis. *H.G. Wells's The War of the Worlds: A Graphic Novel.* North Mankato, Minn.: Stone Arch Books, 2014.

Miller, Ron. *Curiosity's Mission on Mars: Exploring the Red Planet.* Minneapolis: TFCB, Twenty-First Century Books, 2014.

Rusch, Elizabeth. *The Mighty Mars Rovers: The Incredible Adventures of Spirit and Opportunity.* Boston: Houghton Mifflin Books for Children, 2012.

INTERNET SITES

FactHound offers a safe, fun way to find Internet sites related to this book. All of the sites on FactHound have been researched by our staff.

Here's all you do:

Visit *www.facthound.com*

Type in this code: 9781491481066

GLOSSARY

aquifer (AK-wuh-fuhr)—an underground lake or stream of water

crater (KRAY-tuhr)—a hole made when large pieces of rock crash into a planet or moon's surface

engineer (en-juh-NEER)—a person who uses science and math to plan, design, or build

lander (LAND-uhr)—a spacecraft that lands on an object to study the surface

laser (LAY-zur)—a thin, intense, high-energy beam of light

nuclear (NOO-klee-ur)—having to do with the energy created by splitting atoms

orbit (OR-bit)—the path an object follows as it goes around the Sun or a planet

orbiter (OR-bit-ur)—a spacecraft that orbits a planet or other space objects

robot (ROH-bot)—a machine that performs tasks for humans

rover (ROH-vur)—a small vehicle that people can move by using remote control; rovers are used to explore objects in space

sediment (SED-uh-muhnt)—sand and other fine particles eroded and carried by water that settle to the bottom of a body of water such as a lake

telescope (TEL-uh-skohp)—instrument made of lenses and mirrors that is used to view distant objects

BIBLIOGRAPHY

Baker, David. *NASA Mars Rovers: 1997-2013 (Sojourner, Spirit, Opportunity, and Curiosity): An Insight into the Technology, History, and Development of NASA's Mars Exploration Roving Vehicles.* Sparkford, UK: Haynes Publishing, 2013.

Conway, Erik M. *Exploration and Engineering: The Jet Propulsion Laboratory and the Quest for Mars.* Baltimore: Johns Hopkins University Press, 2015.

"Gamma Ray Spectrometer." 2001 Mars Odyssey Lunar and Planetary Lab, the University of Arizona. May 5, 2016. grs.lpl.arizona.edu/home.jsp.

Kaufman, Marc. *Mars Up Close: Inside the Curiosity Mission.* Washington, D.C.: National Geographic, 2014.

"Mars Exploration." NASA. May 5, 2016. mars.nasa.gov.

"Mars Exploration Rovers." NASA. May 5, 2016. mars.nasa.gov/mer/home/.

"Mars Odyssey." NASA. May 5, 2016. mars.nasa.gov/odyssey/.

"Mars Pathfinder." NASA. May 5, 2016. mars.nasa.gov/MPF/index1.html.

"Mars Reconnaissance Orbiter." NASA. May 5, 2016. mars.nasa.gov/mro/.

"Viking Mission to Mars." NASA Facts. May 5, 2016. www.jpl.nasa.gov/news/fact_sheets/viking.pdf.

INDEX